This is Henry's
dinosaur coloring book!

HENRY DIGS DINOSAURS

COLORING BOOK LOADED WITH FUN FACTS & JOKES

C. A. Jameson

Copyright ©2018 C. A. Jameson

Hi, Henry!

HENRY DIGS DINOSAURS is more than just a coloring book. Yes, every page has fun pictures of dinosaurs to color, but there is much more!

It's filled with "*Henry's Fun Facts*" about dinosaurs so you can learn a little while you color. You'll also find funny dinosaur jokes so you can laugh a lot along the way!

Come on, friend, let's go!

Henry's Fun Fact
The word dinosaur means "terrible lizard."

Henry's Fun Facts

Dinosaur fossils (remains) have been found on every continent. Scientists who study fossils are paleontologists.

What do you call a sleeping dinosaur?

A dino-snore!

Henry's Fun Fact
Dinosaurs lived on Earth over 66 million years ago.

Henry's Fun Fact
Dinosaurs were all sizes. Some very huge and some as small as a rabbit.

What is it called when a dinosaur gets a touchdown?

A dino-score!

Henry's Fun Fact
Some dinosaurs were herbivores (plant-eaters).

Henry's Fun Fact
Some dinosaurs were carnivores (meat-eaters).

Henry's Fun Fact
Carnivores were hunters with sharp teeth & claws.

What do you call a dinosaur who eats fireworks?

Dino-mite!

Henry's Fun Facts

Triceratops was a large, slow-moving herbivore very common in what is now the western United States. It ate low growing plants with 800 teeth!

Henry's Fun Facts

Brachiosaurus was a gigantic herbivore with a long neck and small head. It ate plants that were growing high off the ground.

What does a triceratops sit on?

Its tricera-bottom!

Henry's Fun Facts

Tyrannosaurus Rex was a fast-moving carnivore with strong jaws able to crush other animals. Its arms were not useful, but its brain was twice the size of other meat-eaters.

Henry's Fun Facts

Stegosaurus was a large, heavy herbivore very common in western America. It had big, upright plates on its back and a tail tipped with spikes.

What do dinosaurs use to cut wood?

A dino-saw!

Henry's Fun Facts

Ankylosaurus was a large, slow-moving herbivore with little leaf-shaped teeth. It used its tail as a club and had very tough outside armor for protection from Tyrannosaurus Rex and other carnivores.

Henry's Fun Facts

Spinosaurus was a large carnivore with a sail-like form on its back. It was known to eat fish and may have lived both on land and in water.

Where do dinosaurs buy groceries?

At the dino-store!

Henry's Fun Facts

Pterodactyls and other **Pterosaurs** were relatives of dinosaurs, but not dinosaurs. These flying lizards were fish eaters. Birds of today evolved from dinosaurs, and not from **Pterosaurs!**

Henry's Fun Facts

Velociraptors were fast carnivores with long claws and sharp teeth. These dinosaurs, like birds, had feathers, nests full of eggs and hollow bones. But, unlike birds, they did not fly.

Henry's Fun Facts

Dinosaurs roamed Earth for over 150 million years and then mysteriously became extinct. Scientists disagree on the reasons for the disappearance.

Henry's Fun Fact
Dinosaurs became extinct long before the first humans appeared on Earth.

HELP THE DINOSAURS

FIND THEIR YOUNG!

Personalized Books for Children

by C. A. Jameson

Over 100 names available...
Your child is the main character in each book!

Fun Coloring Books and
Storybooks Available About:

Unicorns
Birthdays
Space
Christmas
Easter
Rhymes
Halloween
Science
Valentine's Day
and More!

cajameson.com

Made in the USA
Monee, IL
15 August 2022

11651023R00031